For Hawie whose poetry lights up the world

The Flame of Life

Marguerite Guzmán Bouvard

Marguerite G Bouvard

For Lina Hussein

Published by
Human Error Publishing
www.humanerrorpublishing.com
paul@humanerrorpublishing.com

Copyright © 2018
by
Human Error Publishing
&
Marguerite Guzmán Bouvard

All Rights Reserved

ISBN: #
978-0-9973472-3-4

Cover photo and design by Jacques Bouvard

Remember that you are all people and that all people
are you

Joy Harjo

ACKNOWLEDGMENTS

With gratitude to the magazines in which these poems first appeared:

Time, Tiger Spirit, Water Music, *Epiphany*

My Grandmother's Sheets, *Feila-Festa*

High Noon, The Grace of Solitude, Emmanuel African Methodist Church, After the Storm, *Third Wednesday Press*

The Walk, Miracles, *Story Circle Journal*

Reading the Sky, A Father's Arms, *Louisiana Literature*

Annick, Victory Signs in the Darkness, El Greco, Balance, *Journal of Kentucky Studies*

New Lessons, Chest (*a medical journal*)

Opening Night's Doors, Baalbek, Lebanon, What the Sky Tells Us, Wind, *Greenwich Village Literary Review*

June, the Micro-World, *The Wild Word*

Ana, *The Hawaii Pacific Review*

Borders, *Oracle Fine Arts Magazine*

Opening the Scrolls, Fate, *Passager Magazine*

The Mountain's Homily, *Kerf*

East-West-East, Hidden Stories, Palmyra, This World, Suffer the Little Children, Lifeguards in Lesbos, *Sukoon*

Homs, There Are Two Languages, *San Francisco Peace and Hope*

Makawao Forest, *The Whirlwind*

Stillness, *Tiferet*

A Rising Surf, Presence, Security, Tapestry, *Tell-Tale Inklings #2*

Opening a Door and Earthquakes, *Lady Magazine*

After, Day by Day, Landscape at Agay, *Trajectory*

Another Sunday, Ahihi Kanu Natural Reserve, *Blue Heron Press*

TIME

HISTORY

THE WORLD IN TRANSLATION

THE EARTH'S MANY VOICES

TIME

TIME

On the balcony laundry sways
in the wind, and beyond the railing
is a curving road, triangles of roofs,
a litany of changes. The farm has disappeared.
The farmer no longer takes his daily break
to gaze at the Mt. Blanc with its symphony
of clouds. Trees are replaced like passengers
on a moving train. Ski lifts carry languages
from around the world, a litany
of changes that leave no stories.
But the light rises and fades with the same
rhythm inside these rooms; the white cloth
with its embroidery blue as a summer sky
remembers my mother's hands, over a table
where words gather each day, opening
their petals like saxifrage, buttercups and weeds.
The lamps that accompany us were crafted
in Savoie and in the room where our children
giggled and fought when we turned off
the lights, with the same dresser
that once held our granddaughter's
art projects — the laughter hasn't faded,
nor has the wall hanging of birds that flew
out of my needles or the spotlight that my loved one
nailed on the ceiling to illuminate
its colors, nor the wires snaking around doors
and walls that are the story of his hands.
Here things see and know each other,
the handmade wood table with its array
of fruit, the photos on the mantelpiece above

the fires that warmed us over the years.
Here the light rises and fades with its own
rhythm where we write our own story
and honor the years whirling past
with the steadfastness of love.

MY GRANDMOTHER'S SHEETS

were made in the time when the coach and four
gave way to motors and the Hapsburg Empire
stretched from Western to Eastern Europe
so that home was everywhere.

They were made of the finest linen, edged
with open-work embroidery, skeins of silky flax.
My grandmother carried them to America
after the war as if they were pages

of a cherished book, the ones
I lifted out of a hidden trunk after
my mother died, and contain
my grandmother's stories, a mingling

of Austrian, French and Italian
cradled in the glittering arms
of Trieste's harbor. As I smooth them
over the mattress. I see my grandmother's

house on Via Cavana where orange trees
bloomed in courtyards, where daily life
was a ceremony and the past
had a place of honor at the table.

A LATE MORNING WALK

Right on cue, the elderly couple
park their car on the upper slope
and begin their descent. He is wearing shorts
and binoculars, her flowered dress
flares out to accommodate her bulk.
Their steps are perfectly synchronized,
they have no need for words, their thoughts
crossing easily, the two of them
making a sum greater than the whole.
They are unencumbered now with only their white caps,
a purse sagging against her hip,
and the pleasures of a familiar landscape.
They have made it this far, walking
past the time of the Nazi occupation
when an orange, an egg and butter were as rare
as gold, past the time when they roller skated
in the streets as children because gas
was at a premium in the post-war world.
Maybe she once wore white gloves and a muff.
Maybe he returned from the Algerian War
bruised by memories. Now they are in style
with their visor caps, walking on the edge of eternity
as easily as if they were just crossing the street.

HIGH NOON

It is quiet now, no more trucks
grinding up the road hauling dirt
and gravel, no thunder
of construction, just the birds
calling to each other across
the meadow, the leaves'
quiet songs in the wind, while
the tall row of larches are deep
in meditation, and the low music
of cowbells tells another story.
Time to consider what has been
drowned out, the broken plate
my husband is repairing on the table
laundry spelling a day on the balcony,
and my desk with its own stories,
a pile of books, post-cards
for my granddaughters,
trying to reach words that can hold
the multiples of our being,
and the short story a World War II
veteran sent me, who carries history
in his bones, "a war in which our casualties
for eleven months were three quarters
of a million soldiers" time to remember,
my husband as a young child in a school
occupied by Nazi soldiers who also
speaks the language of war. And time
to celebrate, the sight of my husband's
hands, the way he always repairs
what has been broken, the way our thoughts
find each other without speaking.

THE WALK

"Today I'll let you be the guide," my husband grins like a cat about to corner a bird. I want to show him. I head for the Egyptian restaurant where the same man sits fingering his beads day after day, turn right at the end of the street where a motorcycle is covered with a bright blue plastic cloth. What if the motorcycle were gone, then what?" he asks. "Then there were would be square windows on one side of the street and round ones on the other," I reply. "I want you to understand that Cromwell road is parallel to High Street Kensington. Where is North?" "North is the store window with all the teddy bears," I tell him. In truth, I cannot see left or right, cannot steer myself by maps. "It's simple," he says. "All you have to do is follow a few rules and then you can find your way anywhere." We both can. I am always at home with windows, signs, colors, and the chaos of life along the streets. I slip into them and scenes unfold like pages in the wind. He too is at home everywhere. But they are separate languages, so we argue and spar, spar and argue with the same stubborn spirit. Then we embrace, walking down the street hand in hand, each of us focused on our own horizons.

ONE VILLAGE
for Salif Diabagate

As if they had sprung from the very soil,
the sculptures stand in a semi-circle
on a ridge above the blue-green fields
of Joucas in Provence.

They are tree tall and slender,
iron-sinued and clothed in bark.
They are Africans; the woman with power
in her belly, the man wrapped in his strength

and dignity, children gathered at their feet.
Through their eye holes the sky shimmers,
clouds drift by. Through their open mouths
echo the first songs. They are spirit

marrying flesh, creatures of wind and air.
In their dancing they are the first
twelve people of the world.
Through the folds of their dreaming

flow rivers of clan, nation and tribe.
We are all one village, they sing,
where there is no greater or lesser.
We are nomo, the soul that never dies.

THE WIND'S LESSONS
for Yuko

The wind shifts the direction of ocean currents,
the foam's white calligraphy rushing in
with new episodes that bow us
beneath their weight. It's the wind
that holds our lives in its grip,
yet when we are the most
alone, it suddenly erases distances.
Take the woman who lost her son,
whose sadness sent her spiraling
downwards through months.
But then a friend calls
because her husband's cancer
is whittling him down to bone.
"I am taking care of both of them now,"
she says with a new glow
in her once vacant eyes. She is a mother
again, soothing wounds,
her arms enfolding; remembering
how the shape of our lives changes
in ways we could never see
across the wall of our grief,
how the wind that once tore us apart
also lets in sheaves of light,
and she herself was never lost.

READING THE SKY
for Mary

What do we do when heavy clouds
take possession of the sky,
a majestic movement of dark

continents rising behind clumps
of trees, diminishing
forests, streets, courtyards where children

are playing, trucks that carry
their cargo, for we all have burdens
to carry. I remember the light

piercing a sudden dispersion
of gunmetal gray, cherished moments
that resurrect us from sorrow,

the tall grass conversing
with the wind, the opening pages
of a valley, of a life we reinvented

when one of the roads was shut down.
It's the unfathomable journey
of those continents above us

that reminds us that we need their heavy
darkness to move us forward
in search of light, yet another resurrection.

DAY BY DAY
for Rafe

The real marvelous is in
the extraordinary

and the mundane; the first leaves
budding on the Japanese maple

that holds the promise
of a scarlet blaze. The cardinal's

red flash after winter's
silent skies. And my great nephew's

courage in his grueling journey
through chemotherapy, his shallow

breath, his kindness that spills from
his too short years, the way light

spills through frayed clouds
and cannot be contained.

MIRACLES
for Ariel

We don't speak of miracles,
but of cause and effect,
Nor do we speak

about history although it has cast us
on its shores.
But there are miracles

everyday: the child who entered
this world with eyes that see
our everyday lives

more clearly and who finds beauty
wherever she goes,
awakening us

to our surroundings, a night
without pain, the person who sees
beyond himself and honors

the differences with everyone
he meets, a flower spilling its fragrance
and colors in a bare field.

ANNICK

From early June to October she lives
high up in the mountains
on the Chaine des Aravis
above the Col des Annes, with only a few

farms, a cascade of cows fanning
over pastures. She serves meals
in her small restaurant, in an old sweatshirt,
but dressed in smiles as she swishes

from her kitchen to the tables, she who
has worked there for 40 years, beginning
at the age of 13 when her grandfather
owned the farm. The people at the tables

chatter and comment on the ham,
the sharp taste of alcohol made from
gentians. But she carries wisdom
in her solitude, showing us

that it's not the proud who hunger
for recognition, who tout
their elegance and success,
but the importance of caring

for her aged mother who is ill, the brief
flame of life that is for the love
of family and others, seeing the beauty
of a sunset after a heavy rain.

TAPESTRY

I'm on a plane bound for Boston,
but when I close my eyes,
I am still in London where the front gate
creaks open at 17 Wallgrave Road,

and my daughter and granddaughter
step out to walk at a fast clip,
as they always do, talking
to each other about

small and important events,
and I am walking behind them,
their gestures and profiles so similar
yet different, the way words

compose a sentence. Their long hair
flares in the wind as does their laughter.
They are so absorbed in each other,
their lives intertwined, are a living

tapestry, their heels clicking
their shoulders often making a straight
line since they are the same height.
They are so absorbed in each other;

the years, the silk threads of their
conversations, how my granddaughter
calls her mother when she comes home
late from a party, tells her

the many stories of her day at school
and also about the threads that hang
from the edges, her stepmother's
sharp words, the light and dark
of her father. Then they discuss
the tube strike, my daughter's issues
at work, their moments of joy
and discovery. This tapestry will also

be a flying carpet that will take
each one to different places,
but its silk threads will remain
intertwined, so many pieces of time

and of their lives held together,
a weaving that will never lose
its bloom, the array of rich colors
from each other's heart.

SECURITY

After passport control, we all slip
off pieces of our daily life,
stand with our arms above
our heads to be X-rayed;
Everyone is naked.

But there is yet another
passage. A white-haired woman
carrying her years is being patted
down on her hips, thighs
and back by a security guard;
Everyone is the same.

Then we are released into
our own identities.
Five Hasidic Jews are travelling
through their lives in black,
under black hats with wide rims
that are wings to the Divine.

And two Arab men in jeans
are conversing with each other
in another musical tone.
And a young African American
woman yawns, her body
blooming beneath tight clothes,

while an old man clutches
his briefcase scarred by many
decades, and iPhones hold

gazes like magnets. Then flights
are announced as we scatter and
disperse into other dualities
of certainties and uncertainties.

PRESENCE

Early morning has its routines.
Along the path by the ocean in Maui,
the naupaka bushes' fleshy leaves

are holding the first light. Clouds
of spray burst from the timed
sprinklers, accompanying the runners

that are rested and refreshed. Couples
run in tandem, some pausing
to take photos on their iPhones,

a few holding cups of coffee
or water bottles as they pass by
in a blur focused on their sprints

and conversations. They do not see
the gaunt long-haired man walk by
wrapped in the black plastic

of a garbage bag, without routines
or conversations, wearing the shadow
of loneliness, of undefined days, nights

that have no address. The runners
and this man do not speak
the same language or see his cloak

of misery, yet his presence
has its own dignity, its secret pulse,
and is not drowned by the daily clatter.

THE GRACE OF SOLITUDE

In the airport that is like a city,
crowds around departure gates
come in waves, reshaping themselves
in eddies, opening handbags

and backpacks, families clustering
in the rows of chairs. Yet one person's
presence spells the many facets
of solitude. He seems very short

and thin compared to the others,
yet holds so many decades in his face.
His alligator shoes and cowboy hat
give him a certain flair, although his gait

is slow and he does not speak English.
He carries nothing besides
his years, a quiet dignity
that belies his physical frailty.

We live in a world where belonging
matters, where we are busy, always
in movement. Yet this man's stillness,
and his solitude is a book of memory,

a presence that has no need
of what so many yearn for.
Watching him is seeing a different
measure of time and being.

OPENING NIGHT'S DOORS

Evenings the Mt. Blanc displays its lights,
deep rose blazing, a strip of pure gold
rising above the darkness, when our world

is silenced, and we are reminded
that its dimension is no taller than
the grass, and our passage is brief.

The mountain's language is that
of eagles and hawks, the crash of water
over rocks. Yes, there are airplanes

roaring above, but only for a minute
and minutes are all we have
and must learn to cherish. They fill

the emptiness that can assault us when we least
expect it, the shadow of loneliness,
the memory of the child that graced

our arms, the person who was able
to see what lies beneath our silence,
a sudden burst of understanding.

May each moment be filled
with love and the passion that guides
us for they are our mountains.

VENZONE

After the earthquake
turned Venzone into fields
of rubble, each stone, archway and column
that survived was catalogued

and now the Duomo of Sant Andrea
soars anew. But what holds me
is not the nave rising above me
or the altar glowing

with its stained glass windows,
but walls with swaths of exposed
masonry, shreds of frescos
like wounded flesh,

reminding me of my young friend
struggling across the room
on his walker, and my cousin,
Sandro, his leg severed

by cancer, balanced
on his prostheses, so we can see
how what was lost and what was gained
shine together in these walls.

NEW LESSONS

How much we take for granted,
I reflect,
remembering a long hike with my husband
when I could focus on
the valley unfurling beneath us, each step
as easy as breathing,
and how turning off the light each night
meant sleep, then
greeting the day as if it were an endless expanse.
Now each day is a negotiation
and the hours are few, but I have learned that
few can be many.
I have discovered a world that flees
grief and illness,
but that with friends and my loved one
few can be many.
I have discovered how to reach out
to those we ignore,
the depth of compassion, the hidden cost
of a new kind of learning,
and that despite the static of endless nights,
unpredictable days,
these prisons are not within myself.

THE MICRO-WORLD

There are the corridors of air laden
with pollen, and the nectar drinking bats

and night flowers whose lives
intertwine, the miniature Gentians

that shed their blue light after the snow
has melted, and the first steps a child

takes that are its wings, its first
words opening the door of the world,

and the hand clasping the hand for decades
that pulses with love and understanding.

AFTER

the downpour
pale light,

the astonishment
of mist

flowing up
a mountain road.

A slow river
whose destiny

is air
not the sea,

bypassing
parked cars, pylons

all that is
immobile,

time shimmering
before us.

HISTORY

VICTORY SIGNS IN THE DARKNESS

The young people are sitting in a café
sharing their stories, intimacy,
and red wine, and gathering
at a concert in Bataclan music pulsing

in their veins, and sharing
their excitement at a sport stadium,
another generation enjoying
the simple pleasures

of every day, when suddenly
a burst of explosions shatters
their lives. The massacre was meant
to kill an embrace, music that lifted them

to the sky, and the joy that united
them, by those who invented their
name to draw the disaffected
with false promises, who see

victory in shattered corpses,
the breath of people's screams,
a river of blood, and seek to drown out
the voices of those who do not want

the law of the jungle. But after
the week of sirens and police streaming
through the streets, Paris
regained its voice, as the cover

of Charlie Hebdo shows
a bullet-riddled man spouting
champagne, with the words,
"They have the weapons. Screw them.

We have champagne," and the young
people flock to their cafes again
because nobody tells a French person
what to do, and a powerful voice

demolishes the massacre — a young man
who lost his wife and remains
alone with his tiny son
pronounces a true victory,

"You will never get my hatred.
If God whom you blindly
killed made us in his image,
each bullet in the body of my beloved wife

is a wound in his heart. So I won't give
you the victory of my anger
which would be the same
ignorance that has defined you.

You would like me to sacrifice
Liberty for security. My wife
will accompany my son and I
everyday, and we will meet

in a paradise of free souls.
Everyday my son will answer you

with his happiness and freedom,
and you will not receive his hatred."

RESURRECTIONS

for Philip

After the last and unexpected May
snow, the meadows are glistening
with tall grasses swaying, wild flowers
are spreading their colors, the deep blue
of Bavarian gentians, fragile wood
geraniums, a blazing clump of
buttercups, meadow saffron,
the resurrections we experience on
the roads we travel. My cherished friend
who lost his wife, writing of his love
for her over so many years, only to find
a woman with an open and kind face
who agreed to walk with him, the physician
who took the subway in the middle
of the night to our apartment when
I was a child with a raging fever, who
knew that we could only pay a fragment.
The head of an Artist's Retreat who
noticed that I stayed in my room
when I was mired in depression, yet
carried up every meal for me with utter
kindness until I recovered. If we take
the time to gauge what matters, we will
see splendor in the smallest places,
the sky will open its windows.

EL GRECO

It's the elongated hands that lift us
into the country of deep shadows

and blazing apparitions, fingers
resting upon ancient texts: palms raised

like birds in mid-air, whole bodies
soaring beyond themselves.

St. Francis kneels before us, hands
crossed, his splayed fingers

delicate as new shoots.
St. James the Great still gazes

at what lies beyond our vision,
his many hued cloak swept

by passion's wind,
his light- drenched hand

ferrying us above centuries
of petty quarrels, despicable wars.

ANA

Ana, I have learned to see
the mountain rising behind
you bearing the scars

of your ruined Havana, the sun-struck
panes of your grandmother's window,
staining her hair with their reds

and blues. It smokes with the fever
of burning flesh from mid-night
roundups in the prisons of Moncado.

During a time without mercy
or compassion, Ana, your hands
have cradled children and dreams;

Your country's history rages inside you
and the flight of birds.
You and I have learned how power

sprouts like kudzu, drowning
the tender fields. Speaking of this
across the table where the hours

pause over tea, our words
become grass springing back
defiant flowers.

HISTORY

The wind has its own destination
and we are caught
in its web; those of us who become ill,
teetering on the edge, learn

to negotiate each day in a different
landscape, and the Rohingyas,
Muslims fleeing from
oppression, who have become

a floating people on the Andaman sea
among countries who refuse
them access, while they dream
of a destination where

they can pray, work, bear the children
they are forbidden to have
in Myanmar, and not remain stateless.
To survive means traveling

through a storm on an unmarked
road, learning a new language,
and bearing witness
to the initiations of life,

a story of courage that is not
in our history books where militias,
dictators, and heroic leaders
fill the pages.

A FATHER'S ARMS

for Kevin Lucey

once held   a son
who returned   from war
stalked   the streets in camouflage   gun
at his side drank   to forget
his buddy   torn apart   by a land mine
the constant   sounds of rocket
propelled grenades   explosively
formed projectiles   and then
silence   and with it   fear
of what is   to come   terror
that won't   subside
the high-pitched screech
and crack   invading   his nightmares
the slam   of a door   telling him
that he's still   in the desert   will always be
in danger   even when his father
holds him close   an invisible
mist blurs   his street   his house
what doesn't   evaporate   are the times
he sat in a humvee   one foot
in front of another   hands   behind
his back   to protect them
from being   blown off   memories
his father's arms   could not
erase   with a faithful   constant love
could not heal   what is broken
convince   his son   that he's not
a stranger   if he stays   prevent him
from stepping   out of time.

BORDERS

Morning, sloughed off dreams,
buzz saws through my open window

    alternating with the chatter of birds,
    the quiet journey of clouds writing

their messages of what's to come,
with their dark undersides. Shadows

    entering my room with the calligraphy
    of light. The border between night

and day, and the border between
Southern Texas and Mexico;

    with immigrants streaming in from Guatemala,
    Honduras, and el Salvador, women and children

who want safety from violent gangs,
an open door, who carry hope

    in their empty hands,
    for a reunited family, for a place

to live, to walk into tomorrow,
on our unfamiliar streets

    where the air is not divided
    and our hearts have no borders.

SEASONS

They are all intertwined on this lush green
slope; the two- note song and the questioning
note of black birds, punctuated by raucous
crows, the din of construction far above,

then a plane's brief hum in a country
where strikes have closed airports, like
so many other countries in the west where
the young people cannot find jobs

and take to the streets, where in Boston
as in so many other cities, young women
like Maria Vasquez is working
seven days a week in two jobs

with no hope for the future, college
graduates who return home because they cannot
find work, or Paula who moved to Switzerland
to complete a master 's degree, her dreams

of the vanishing world of the heart
and commitment, where the word love
has disappeared and men who leaned
into her life vanish for no reason,

and my husband and I count our many
blessings, a decades long marriage, jobs
that lasted, a roof over our heads,
words that have disappeared like "choice,"

"a future," we could count on, a journey
through good times and bad where the road
didn't bifurcate and the hope we traced
out together, the flowers of long years bloomed.

THE LEXICONS THAT DIVIDE US

"All those immigrants pouring over
our borders," a woman's snaps, her face
brimming with anger. But we are not statistics.
We are born with names, held together
by the bonds of family and hope.
Twelve-year old Claudia who was held
for months in a U.S. Border Patrol Station,
the room crowded and frigid, where she
was hungry, thirsty, without the voices
of her family and friends, just the border
guards berating her -- hanged herself
from the shower curtain rod in a bathroom.
We live in a country where language
and perceptions divide us. Like so many
children fleeing violence in El Salvador,
and seeking asylum as minors, Jose
became so terrified of being detained
by Immigrations and Customs Enforcement,
he decided to return to his country
and give up his asylum case. Six months
after he arrived, he was killed by armed
strangers, his loss leaving a gaping wound
in his father's heart. For too many of us
the word "immigrant "means taking our jobs,
and transforming our country, even though
they are invisible, working in farms,
or low paying jobs, their families being torn
apart by deportations. And the word
"refugee" just makes us turn away.

EMMANUEL AFRICAN METHODIST CHURCH

The parishioners who are torn by grief
are holding hands in the aisles,
and embracing each other in the courtroom,
forgiving the white man who stares

blank faced in silence, who wanted
to maim their congregation with his gun,
killing nine -- and are united
by the light of their love and faith,

for their church has a long history: the path
started in a dark wood by Denmark Vesey,
in 1822, a slave whose road
to hope was studded with nails,

and ended in a noose, the glow of fires
that burned so many black churches
sparked by hatred and ignorance.
Vesey's life was a word that remained

in the ashes and rubble and in the hymns
throughout centuries, in the radiant
souls who trek through their history
with the loss of their loved ones,

the shackles of cruelty and violence,
denied space or a voice. Yet their light
is not dimmed within a world
that refuses to honor our diversity.

TAMIR RICE

He was just a twelve-year old boy playing with a toy gun,
perched on a swing, free from school, lost in his thoughts
and dreams, enjoying the moment. He was just a boy.
I remember telling my son that he couldn't have a toy
gun, so he picked up a stick saying, bang, bang. But it wasn't
the toy that Tamar was playing with, he who wished no harm
to anyone, had a mother who loved him, cousins who lived
a few blocks away, but the color of his skin that made
the policeman shoot him until he died. Do we really believe
the Creator is only white? Have we never seen an
unexpected rainbow after the rain shower? Some of us
wonder why ignorance wins so often. But there is a small
place in the park where Tamir stood that will always be there,
an invisible spot that is holy because it holds the innocence
of a child who had a heart, a soul, and a family who loved him.

A NEVER ENDING STORY

Late morning on a mountain slope
in the middle of summer where the only
sounds are the back and forth
twittering of birds, where clusters

of billowing white clouds spell
more sunshine and remain suspended
as if time were frozen and silence
were a part of the world we live in,

not the crowded streets where Eric Garner
died in a police chokehold for selling
cigarettes, or the car that was stopped
by the police for a supposedly broken

tail light, and while Philando Castile
reached in his pocket for his drivers license
fell back dripping with blood in front of
his girl friend and her four-year-old

daughter, love and hatred intertwined,
the love of a four-year-old girl saying,
"Mommy, it's going to be okay,"
and the inner enemy of hatred wanting

mirrors to reflect only oneself, to own
the streets, strip them of different skin
colors — the darkness of disdain, and
the light in a little child's tender voice.

OPENING THE SCROLLS

In a single week the giant
statues of Buddha towering
against the Afghan Hills,
folding millennia in their calm gazes

were smashed to rubble
by the Taliban. The world's newspapers
quivered with indignation
as if history's scrolls

were never stained by fists
razing temples and torching
holy books, as if there were never
the silencing of gongs and bells

or new markings as in the back alley
of a forgotten town where a child
fills a rusty can with soil
because she believes a green stalk

will appear, because nobody
can destroy her longing
for what she cannot see
or for the spirit that beckons her.

THE MOUNTAIN'S HOMILY

The single piercing chime
of a blackbird and the responding chorus
opens the doors of our hearts
and minds to epiphanies, while the nations
of clouds break apart and come
together. The one note of an ancient
truth in the silence of the peaks'
citadels, in the stillness of roads without
trucks, tractors or tanks, or the madness
of conquest and oppression,
echoes in the light drenched robes
of the evergreens, awakening us to love,
a passageway to both sides of time.

BALANCE

The clouds have their own messages:
the four directions of wind,
their calligraphy becoming a series

of stretched lines, spelling
changes, and there can be both,
the cursive beauty in front

of the harbinger of what is to come,
like the balance in our lives,
the pain that we fear can awaken

us to understanding, connect us to different
languages and countries, and the news
that once clamored with its torrents

is nor longer distant, and darkness
summons light as we gaze at starlight
in the most unexpected places.

ANOTHER SUNDAY

is one of silence, the holy water of rain
that blesses trees and meadows, the absence
of words that wound like swords and the chimes
are bells ringing as horses move across
the untainted grass. The rain tells us
that we are drops of water in the cloud whitened
sky, that if we listen to the beating
of our hearts, two becomes one, if we listen
to a stranger, two becomes one. And the meadow
with its green air tells us that we are each
enfolded with its blades of grass, blessed by the earth
who is our mother. In the silence we are all
faced with, we enter our interior where
there is history with its conflicts and discords
but where tensions can dissolve and the continents
are joined, where one is many and where
time has left its messages for us to contemplate.

THE WORLD IN TRANSLATION

EAST-WEST-EAST

Refined ceramic bowls, vases,
and decorative plates of all sizes trace
a history of the Middle Ages that spans
the Mongolian invasion of Iran

and wars raging throughout
those centuries, yet the Mamelukes
in Syria and Cairo sponsored exquisite
tiled mosques, and Anatolia commissioned

beautifully crafted monuments.
What remains from surges of populations
on the move and changes of Caliphs
are ceramic plates where birds

fly in place and religions are juxtaposed
on tiles; the six pointed star of David
and the eight pointed star
with a lotus flower, tiles of Mary and Joseph

created during the Ottoman Empire,
while multicolored tiles with inscriptions
were fashioned for the entrance
of Hagia Sophia. These precious works

were fired and glazed with the care
in which illuminated manuscripts
were crafted, and traveled quietly
without us realizing that cultures

have no borders, that ceramicists
from Venice and France came to study
Islamic art with its intricacy
and the fluency of pulsing flowers,

branches, radiating deep purples,
greens, yellows and blues,
drawing us in and leaving
behind centuries of discord.

HOMS

that wove centuries
in its buildings and mosques
where people greeted each other
and dawn blessed
Sunni, Shiite, and Christian,
Homs, the ancient city
of light and outstretched hands
where skeletons of buildings
teeter and nameless bodies
lie beneath the rubble
of darkness, where there is no
end, and conferences abroad are filled
with empty phrases as Jihadis
stream in who do not speak
the language -- yet a father
lifts a small child from the remains
of barrel bombs who survived,
and stands alone above the ruins
with their arms intertwined
in an embrace, where the self-proclaimed
killers can never vanquish love.

BAALBEK LEBANON

A man is curled up on the sidewalk,
sleeping, while passersby
are absorbed in their conversations
as they stroll to the café

around the corner, Here
there is no shelter
for the Syrian refugee who rests,
with only a small bundle

at his side but who carries
the times he sat at the table
with the cup of tea his wife
served him, the touch

of her hand, the moonlight
on their bed, the bird song
that greeted him at dawn,
crossing the street on an ordinary

day, and the sudden explosions,
and fusillades, a tangle of screams
and wailing in a city
of ruins, of fragments

from so many centuries,
and then a pause, a silence,
like no other in a war
that will always live inside him.

HIDDEN STORIES

On the upper slopes of La Giettaz
patches of snow linger even when the sun
is high. But in the wall of boulders,
granite and schist stretching skyward,
a small but dense carpet of pale rose
wildflowers have emerged from
a crack, petals calling out
with rounded leaves that are thick
and dark green, holding their stories
while in a world struggling with the loss
of so many species, two monarch butterflies
flutter above the flowers,

and in the tsunami
of statistics as refugees cross
the Mediterranean in crowded and unsafe
boats, we count the numbers
who have drowned, and too many countries
clamor against open borders while only a few
manage to avoid telling the refugees
that they do not belong.

Denial and thunderous silence
fill the air, and blind us to the future
of how adolescent Syrian girls are able
to weave a path beyond the noise
of discord and through the cracks of statistics:

Muntaha, who began painting at home before
the war tells us at the age of thirteen,

"Art inspires peace, encourages
us to be kind to each other," Fatima,
who now is in school after years
of longing reminds us, "education
is the most important thing in life,
knowledge is a weapon," and sixteen
year old Bassina remembers how
a pharmacist in Syria helped
the injured now works in a pharmacy
and studies at night.

If those of us whose
life passes by so fast, disputing
the loss of species, and the response
to borders, paid attention to the young
who do not fit into their schemes,
they would understand the hearts of others,
and how the war torn bring us hope
in tender hands that kindle sunrise.

PALMYRA

the cradle of ancient civilizations
where monuments inspired by
Greco-Romans and Persians
hold up the sky, and time

stands still, when my hands can't
reach out or encircle the children
who were unable to flee
 or to rebuild the walls of bombed out

houses, are unable to light
candles of hope when night and day
are reversed, and a woman who was a wife
and mother lies on the cobbled street

her blood leaving its marks,
while the blind-hearted man
who destroyed so many names
and faces turns away with his rifle

cocked, believes that he is cleansing
Syria in a holy war, cloaked
in ideology, exchanging
a slogan for his soul.

THIS WORLD

Behind my face is another
face that nobody sees.
It carries so many absences:
the fear of a child who has crossed
the border, her father cutting
a barbed wire fence between Syria
and Turkey, Falah, his wife
and their baby daughter changing their
residence for the twelfth
time in Iraq where life turns
on the axis of a roulette, and borders
crop up within other borders, and the cascade
of shouts are not intelligible,
where we have become fugitives
on the streets we once crossed
to buy a loaf of bread or to visit a neighbor,
streets that reflected sunlight
are now filled with wails, its trees
devoid of branches, its doors clanging
in the wind while walls buckle.
This shattered world can only
be pieced back together with
the words brother, sister, friend.

SUFFER THE LITTLE CHILDREN

It took me too many days to muster the courage
to pick up the newspaper with the front-page photo
of Abu Anas Ishara's three-year-old daughter
half naked, her sweet face held in a scream
of extreme pain and confusion
from yet another chemical shell
that landed on her house
enveloping her parents and her newly born
sister in dust and foul smelling
smoke. Her scream remains
without answer, with no arms
to hold her, no medical care in Marea*. Her skin
carries the map of a country that pundits
discuss from afar and disagree
among themselves according to their
own needs. But her scream will not
go away. Her pain will travel
like the clouds sweeping across
the sky and when it finds the open
chambers of a heart, it will be bathed
in tears, it will be answered by
a mother's loving voice.

* Marea is an agricultural village in Syria

SYRIA

I carry a country with me
that is new to traveling, families
trekking with their towns
and villages in the bundles

on their back, traveling with
sunshine streaming through
their window, the voices
of neighbors, a door that opened

into a day filled with promises.
a child rushing in after school,
and a table with the aroma
of fresh bread, cheese and olives,

traveling in a time that is not
predictable, a road within
a road, within a road that seems
endless, where even the word

now is in a book with its pages
in a foreign language,
and the word home is a cloud
in a whirling wind.

A RISING SURF

Today the surf is pounding against the rocks
sending up a spume of shattered waves
like the surf of Syrian refugees
from the Mediterranean landing
in crowded rubber rafts in Lesbos, Greece,
and Lampedusa, Italy, or walking
between Croatia, Serbia, and Austria,
the roads overflowing with endless rows
of families carrying young children
And their few possessions, a flood
of humanity surging towards an unknown
destination, hoping for a Noah's Ark
to lift them above barrel bombs,
clorine and sulfur mustard, blister agent
shells, only to find barbed wire
walls, with police arrayed behind them,
countries who do not wish to see
their homogeneity interrupted or defiled,
And then a country with open doors
who wants them to lives beneath a sky
where clouds are not torn asunder
but filled with luminous stars, roofs,
a patch of earth where children can play
and fill the air with laughter
where the common language
is acceptance, hope, a myriad
of different voices.

THE PROMISED LAND

In the forest, a tree
has fallen, its huge roots

radiating so many severed tendrils
revealing that was once

invisible, is like the country
now throbbing in Kalid's new life;

an uncle, brothers, cousins,
the shattered streets of Aleppo

still filled with memories;
the warm hearth, the mosque where

he prayed, the room
where his little daughter was born,

but now chatters happily
in a new language because he

and his wife are living
in another country that is a desert

where his voice and thoughts
have no echo. People rush by

on the busy sidewalks as he looks
out of his window and prepares

for his day on what feels
like another planet.

EARTHQUAKES

In Amartice, centuries old houses,
are crushed with only a crooked bell tower
left of a church. Throughout central
Italy, towns known for their exquisite beauty

and as tourist attractions collapse
as the earth suddenly shifts and cracks,
so much destroyed in a few minutes.
But people are busy helping

each other, working throughout
the night, to locate survivors, setting up
tents and cots. The world is riveted.
Journalists are collecting

stories, while in Aleppo there are searing
earthquakes caused by bunker bombs
that rain down day after day.
A five- year old boy covered

with the dust and small remnants
of shattered buildings is seated and staring
straight ahead, frozen in time.
His eyes are blank, he has no words

for his shock and cannot speak in
a landscape that is covered with rubble.
He is on another planet that is strange
to him while the physicians

from a bombed hospital are sorting
out whom they can help, the little girl
who lost her arm, small children
lying in gurneys from yet another field

of beauty, but one that is hidden, the petals
of innocence and sweetness drooping,
throughout a city which is no longer
a city that once held the glory of centuries.

LIFEGUARDS IN LESBOS

patrol the water for sinking boats crowded
with refugees, and daily experience
the horror of lifting out a child
with no legs, a man who died

of a heart-attack when he was rescued.
But one of them decided to help
a little girl, Yara, recover from her
fear of the deafening, tumultuous

sea; the screams of a cousin as he
disappeared beneath the sudden
slap of a wave, the loss of her
father's gentle voice, and then

the arrival in a strange place that tore
at her memories where there are
no small consolations like a grandmother's
smile, and lives with her mother

in a tent teeming with other people.
The lifeguard took Yara to the calm part
of the Aegean that was like a mirror
and held her above it in his arms

like a terrified little puppy, spilling
drops of water on her head, a few
at a time. A half-hour later, he added
more drops, then handfuls of water

until finally, Yara was wading with him
and splashing. He created an island
of hope within an island overwhelmed
with thousands of refugees and too few

resources, a moment that was a luminous
unburdening for him and for Yara.
Holding her in his arms, he healed
a world that is besieged by trauma.

THE WORLD IN TRANSLATION

People are walking in droves from Daraya
in Syria, a forced departure from the graves
of their loves ones, the memories of family
and neighborhood gatherings, the prayers
and festivities during Eid. The town will
empty as the crowds move towards
unknown streets, doors without names.
They walk through a torrent of alien
voices, the gunfire's staccato, sudden
explosions only a meter away,
a check point of soldiers demanding
information, and sending them to different
places, but they are carrying more than
their bundles, more than their
fear. They are carrying their hearts
that hold the pages of their lives,
paths that were severed but which
the deluge of blank pages
and metallic voices cannot destroy.

WHAT CONNECTS US

in this world where we are arranged by languages,
where faith has so many different names, enfolding
us in words that lift us and soar or the anger
of bombs, little children wearing suicide vests because
they were ordered to do so, while children on the other side
of the world are playing ball or holding crayons
in their hands, a freshly baked cookie. Everyone has
their own story, like Leila during a never ending
war in Aleppo whose house had no electricity
and was lit by candles, where the light of hope
darkened as she sat blindfolded with the cold metal
of a gun pressed against her forehead, a voice ordering
her to leave her home or else. But Leila received
one year in our country to work for a masters degree,
but then where? Yet she applauds when
her two-year old son Ahmed lifts a wooden number
and says "nine" with triumph. It's not a matter
of languages, dialects or borders that move back
and forth around the world, how some of us wear
the masks of anger or the pride of their position.
We all live in the world of grief, fear, moments
of wonder and discoveries, in the love that brings
us all together regardless of the barriers
that we construct.

WHITE HELMETS

The streets throughout Syria are lined
with sagging buildings, crumbling walls,
the darkness of endless bombing.
But in the middle of the rubble, a man
wearing just a white construction helmet
to protect himself, runs while gently carrying
a wounded little girl in his arms to bring
her to safety. He is one of the many who race
towards the bombs even though Bashir el-Assad's
forces engage in "double tapping"
to strike them, yet they dig through crushed
buildings to rescue a person who was buried
underneath and is crying out. These men
give their lives to save every single one
of the wounded, even fighters from Nusra,
or Assad's military forces. Yet Raed Saleh,
the head of Syria's Civil Defense, the White
Helmets, flew to the U.S. to receive an award
only to be turned away, and responded,
"In any airport, the treatment we get as Syrians
is different." There are two views, two scenes:
one is the political jockeying between Iran,
Russia, Assad, and the U.S., and their endless
military attacks; the other is one of tenderness
and strength driven by the simple belief from
the Qur'an "to save one life is to save humanity."

THERE ARE TWO LANGUAGES

in this country, one is made of slogans,
as would be candidates garner
space in the media, traveling throughout
the country to create fear

of what they call "the other."
Then there is a young
Muslim woman Mona Haydar
who set up an "ask a Muslim" stand

on a busy street offering
free coffee and a doughnut
to passersby who want to know
about her faith. She opened the door

to love, reached out beyond
the boundaries we set up
and the slogans, that bombard us
to draw upon fear, hatred

and misunderstanding.
Opening that door, a young woman
showed us how one person
with a giving heart can make

the world a better place where
we can move beyond our differences
and rejoice together, understanding
the true meaning of life.

THE EARTH'S MANY VOICES

MAKAWAO FOREST

is where silence has many
voices, where we are surrounded
by life and death and there is beauty

here in the death we are so afraid of,
striations of color and texture
from the torn bark of a fallen pine,

and shoots of leaves rise
shimmering from a downed
trunk, is where like the indigenous people

of the world, we walk with the past,
present and future intertwined,
the message of roots

wandering above ground
that greet every step, their journey
has its own language, reminding us

that we are part of it, is where
our whole body thinks and
the forest is a cathedral whose

arches lift our souls, whose music
is quiet reflection and whose aisles
lead us to a new understanding.

AHIHI KANU NATURAL RESERVE

Here the jumbled stones are rounded by their travels in the
ocean, stones whose journeys may have begun in the stars,
an aged mesquite all furrows and lines, tall, dignified, rising
up in its eminence with the wisdom of centuries, the sudden
surges of yellow grasses from the lava reminding us that
the creation moves forward with a power that lies beyond
us, the eerie creaking of the top branches, the outline of
what was once a Hawai'ian dwelling, and always the mur-
muring of the surf telling us its stories --- there are voices
all around us, even in the colors of the sky, the soft violet-
mauve this dusk that speaks of tranquility in our shadowed
world.

MAPHINA LUTA, Chief of Dakota Oglala

After a painting by George Caitlan

His face has no mask like the Belagaana*
but is as open as the plains,
holds so many stories, has the strength
of the forests and his people.
His luminous eyes bear
a deep sorrow, carries a future
that has no place for the Oglala;
their history, the land where they walked
among the messages of eagles,
visions that come in solitude
and in silence, and the voices,
the spiritual dances on an earth
they hold sacred. His name is Red Cloud
because his people know that earth
and sky are one, what they need
to flourish. He is a witness, standing
before a different language, its ambiguous
thoughts, a journey that was never
anticipated, for which there is no medicine,
no ceremonies, now filled with shadows
in his knowing heart.

*White men

STILLNESS

Le Col des Annes, Le Grand Bornand,
le Col de la Colombière are wrapped in dense
clouds and the mountains

take precedence. Behind the clouds,
a faint row of trees, softened lines
of roofs, steeples, forests,

a vast landscape like a Chinese painting.
The speeding cars, gatherings
of tourists are replaced

by a stillness where we are not
the center. For a moment the headlines
disappear; the wars in Iraq

and Syria. For a moment
I am back at a conference of Cherokee
women speaking of peace

and care of the land that is the core
of our being, reminding me to revere
the mysteries of earth and sky.

SHON-TA-YE-GA (LITTLE WOLF)

After a portrait by George Catlin

is the earth walking, a row of eagle feathers
flaring on the back of his head,
for eagles always bring messages

from afar. He wears a necklace of bear claws
since the bear is the mother who once
carried the earth on her back.

His long turquoise earrings carry land
and sky, because the land and his people
flow together dreaming,

and the bracelets on his upper
arm remind us that life is a circle.
Colored lines are painted on his face

that spell his role and that of the Ojibwa.
His lore is vast and deep,
carried though centuries, for he knows

the language of trees, talking rivers,
the whispering of sacred rocks, how to go
out in solitude to receive

visions that will guide his people.
But the expression on his
majestic face reveals a deep sorrow,

portents of a troubled future
that will change his nation
in ways he cannot fathom.

MELT WATER

Waterfalls echo, their eddies scoring the edges of streams with currents like tines, rushing faster than wind, sending up curls, as a script from the Qur'an, broad swaths taking over the gravel, widening its path, carrying light on its skin, one side of the wash twirling like dervishes around a bed of stones, on the other side, strands of light vibrate. It drips from the mountainside with the notes of a piccolo, its sheen illuminating the wall of bare rock, and from the green stalks projecting out of scree, melody of the oboe. Water music strikes the air louder than the jangling of cowbells on the upper meadows. In spring, it reclaims the earth, reminding us that we too have come from its depths like the First Peoples who climbed out of fire and water to enter this world.

WHAT THE SKY TELLS US

Today the sky has drawn
its curtains, the wind is holding
its breath. The mountain does not
wish to see the splendors

of its meadows disappear or hear
the trilling of birds drowned out
by the drone of chainsaws, the thud
of falling trees. It does not want

to witness a land bereft
of its constellations of larch, pines,
birches, plane and linden
covered with asphalt, rows

of chalets and apartment houses.
The sky withdraws its cerulean
blue, its drifting clouds, the light
it sheds where meaning lies

on that which cannot
be owned and the paths made
by our footsteps. The real village
lies in our hearts that are the rooms

of our loved ones, where our
souls open their windows
to see a star, the beauty of flowers,
the grass flaming in early spring.

FATE

On the slope before me some trees
burgeon with rich robes, thick
and glowing with such majesty,
while among them branches are almost
naked and weathered like the aspen
that has become almost transparent,
like my town decked with new elegant
houses, and its grocery store with a bin
for donations of food. Fate, luck, events
are so frail, and we remain divided
by the blindness of splendor, the kingdom
of plenty, and the stories of loss,
their shuttered voices.

WATER MUSIC

The ocean has its own scales:
vibratos of surf against rocks,
cliffs, blow holes, glissando

of coves bringing us
distance, the rhythm of its journey,
surrounding us with its symphonic

presence, a curtain of clouds
sweeping past, reminding us that we are only
intermittent visitors, no more

than a blade of grass or a hibiscus
among bare branches, held
by time before eternity.

TIGER SPIRIT

She who is swift on earth and in water,
swimming kilometers in minutes,

and against the tide, follows the texts
of stillness and surprise,

reclining in the shade of a ruined temple
like a priestess or pouncing on a huge crocodile

as he dozes on a river bank,
then disappearing through the trees

without disturbing a single branch or twig.
Her eyes penetrate

the narrow corridors of our lives, asking
where did the light flee?

WIND

Swishing through pines like the steady crash
of waterfalls

Fraying a dense bank of clouds

Hurling me into the vastness
of someone's heart

Wafting the scent of Lindens
from Senosecchia

A loom that is never stilled

A flock of leaves singing.

AFTER THE STORM

the snow has its own language,
gracing the outstretched limbs
of linden, pin oaks, sugar maples, clothing
the length of the hemlocks and spruce
so that they move closer, take
their own space, a scene once
obliterated by our traffic
and our many differences. The snow
leaves clean slates on roofs,
the edges of sidewalks, stretches
of concrete so we become aware
that we are visitors on this earth
and remain quiet, hearing the snow
tell the stories of trees intertwined
with starlight, the secret work
of roots recording moisture
and drought, hear the ancient music
of becoming, the holy scripts
that were written before us
connecting us to every leaf, wing
and branch, praising the beauty,
and grandeur we pass by.

JUNE

The stillness of early June;
just the trilling of birds
above silent meadows, the green light
of Archangel Raphael, and the trees
silent watch with their scrolls
of leaves spelling creation,
and the clear syllables
of birds, their tones etching
the crystalline air.
A meditation on being.

OPENING A DOOR

A woman sitting by the ocean
was watching
the sunset as if music was welling
up inside her and
she was having a dialogue with
light, her face uttering
wonder, a flash of amazement as if
someone had spoken
to her with kindness and serenity,
and she had slipped
out of her days into the arms
of a wider life.

RENEWAL

A day so bright and still, a day so warm
after weeks of heavy rainfall and cold
winds keeping the cows inside
the barns, the tall uncut grasses
of the meadows flattening and spoiling
so there will be no hay for the winter.
Seasons no longer follow each other
in a procession and new ways
of calculating gain and loss knock
at our doorsteps while on the other side
of the world, mountain slopes
no longer keep their mantle of snow
and water has been reduced so that
we now use paper plates and are
told lawns must no longer exist,
because wildfires rage through forests
and towns. There was a time when
the forests burgeoned and were
healing -- before pesticides, there was a time
before the unpredictable weather
smothered monarch butterflies while herons,
swallows, and blackbirds' inner magnets
now steer them to trouble, but even though
so few of us agree to be accountable,
there is the Hopi vision that in the world
of the distant future there will be bright
and still days, enough time to till the soil
and clear the meadows. Ferns, wild flowers,
clumps of bushes, and even trees
will sprout from the cracks in the mountains'

highest rocks, we will celebrate
the rainbow of our different colors and spell
tomorrow with a different language.

LANDSCAPE AT AGAY

By Armand Guillaumin

A pale sky reflects the earth; swaths
of green light, muted
lavender rays, while the rocks

flame, its oranges not a sunset
but the earth speaking its many
different voices,

the burgeoning olive groves
singing in the wind
are flickering candles lighting

our way, and the sea, its dark
currents, its foam galloping
on its endless journey,

telling us that history
is a fire that keeps renewing itself,
the earth a prophet.

Marguerite Guzmán Bouvard has published 21 books, including 9 books of poetry and numerous books in the fields of human rights, women's rights, illness, grief and social justice. Her poetry and essays have been widely anthologized and her poetry books have won the Quarterly Review of Literature Award and the MassBook Award for Poetry. She has received grants for her poetry from the Puffin and Danforth foundations.